HUSTLE UP AND START YOUR OWN T-SHIRT BUSINESS

STEPHANIE STEPHENS

Stephanie Stephens

Copyright © 2018 Stephanie Stephens

All rights reserved.

ISBN-13: 978-1722243623

Stephanie Stephens

Preface

Thank you for purchasing hustle up start your t-shirt business and congratulations on taking the first step towards your future as an entrepreneur. You will find this book to be a great resource that you can

Stephanie Stephens

use over and over and share with other people how to start a t-shirt business. I started my own t-shirt business Bleszing Clothing and the spring of 2017 at the time I didn't know anything about how to start a t-shirt business or the fashion industry this was a great experience for me I will say it was a lot of hard work. As I

Stephanie Stephens

continue to grow my business I found a lot of people started reaching out to me asking how can they start their own business so this book is for everyone that has a dream of being a t-shirt entrepreneur business owner I wish you much success on your journey to starting your own t-shirt business.

Stephanie Stephens

Introduction

Have you got an idea or always wanted to start your own t-shirt business I have created the perfect guide for you to start your t-shirt business. A lot of people were asking me how to start a t-shirt business and what made me want to start. The reason I wanted to start was because I wanted to do something to encourage and inspire others so my first t-shirt business was a Christian t-shirt line call Bleszing Clothing the brand was created to uplift and Inspire anyone through fashion. So, I have taken all my experiences and knowledge to help others start their own t-shirt business and this book will give you

Stephanie Stephens

step by step of becoming the next big thing starting a t-shirt line is not as easy as it may sound it takes a lot of dedication and hard work the best thing is that once you start you will fall in love with the process. The best advice I can give is to just start, stay focus, set goals and in no time, you

Stephanie Stephens

will have your own business. So, let us get started already!

Table of Content

1. Develop your interest
2. Find your niche
3. Carry out your research
4. Map out plans
5. Set your Goals and Objectives
6. Determine your Budget
7. Branding
8. Drop Shipping
9. Advertising and marketing
10. Pricing
11. Make Sales

Stephanie Stephens

Chapter 1

DEVELOP YOUR INTEREST

Stephanie Stephens

It is very important first of all that you don't even consider venturing into any long-term business if you are not able to develop a great interest in it. Every business has its point of challenges and bottleneck; however, it is the interest that you have in it that keeps you going.

Sure, you may not have to like what you're doing if we're talking about one-off million-dollar transactions like selling gold, but if you're having a t-shirt business, it's something that lasts longer and therefore loving what you do is a must.

Stephanie Stephens

If you don't have the interest, you simply have to develop it by convincing yourself of the latter advantages and benefits of venturing into it.

So, just like in every other business, developing your interest is the first thing to do before engaging in a T-shirt business.

How then will you develop the interest?

Like it is said above, try to see the benefits the T-shirt business boasts. Also, read as much as possible about the business (I guess you're doing that right now). Create the passion for everything T-shirt.

Stephanie Stephens

Chapter 2

FIND YOUR NICHE

Stephanie Stephens

It can't be told if there are other businesses that can flourish without the perfect niche, but definitely, the T-shirt business is totally excluded. You have to find your niche before you can make good plans. Now, let's define what niche is. Niche is your target audience. It is a highly focused, specific type of people that you want to sell your products to. You must keep it in mind that you cannot sell to everyone, you will just get frustrated. Therefore,

Stephanie Stephens

finding a perfect, precise, and productive niche will help you.

For example, "children" is not yet a good niche for your T-shirt business, because we have many types of children on this planet, neither is "teenagers". It's not specific enough. However, "male teenagers aged 14-18 who love Dolce & Gabbana" is better. Having a niche means you have drawn a clear picture of your market. From what they like to wear, to what designs they love, to what color they would want, to what's in vogue for their class, to what they can spend their money on.

Stephanie Stephens

For real, you now know the importance of finding a niche, but the difficult task now is actually in identifying them. It is not something entirely easy to do, but also, it is not something any impossible. Here are some steps:

1. Whom Do You Want to Do Business With?

You need to fully define who you will like to have transactions with. Are the other businessmen or customers? If you plan to do the T-shirt business for long, you must make sure you're dealing with those who you love dealing with.

2. Identify Your Ready Market

For every business, there is a ready market. You are now left with identifying it. What group of people do you know? Are they politicians? Are they teenagers? What would get their interests? What design will they love?

3. Research the Ones Who Are Willing (and Not Willing) to Spend

No matter how hot your T-shirt designs are, some people can never spend so much on it. For example, men aged over 55 with income less than $30.000 dollars will most likely not be ready to buy funny T-shirts that cost more than $25. With this situation, you must either try to make the T-shirts cheaper or go for men with higher income.

4. Find out in What Niche You Can Still Be Unique

Ask yourself, what can be different and unique to my business? Think of the customization, ordering process, packaging, marketing.

5. Test Your Niches

After series of thinking, the best way for you to find which niche suits the most is testing your niche. You can do a mock-up design and post it online. **Placeit, Creative Market** (There are many sites that do this.)

Chapter 3

CARRY OUT YOUR RESEARCH

You cannot dive into the clothing industry without ensuring you're totally knowledgeable about it. You have to get familiar with the totality of how the business works. This can be done by reading about how other brands became successful and also, gathering insider info from past brand owners interview. You should read as many possible T-shirts business books and also listen to as many possible T-shirts business podcasts because they are the files that will sharpen you for the work. Research on the designs your target group loves the most. You need too, to research the finances needed for the business. You must understand what it takes to startup.

Also, one other thing you have to research about is your competition. It is very vital for you to understand what companies, and how many of them you're competing with. This, you must do, to find out if there's still a room for you in that market. If in your locality, there are already five businesses specialized in the Sports T-shirts, you have to find out if you can join them and still achieve your goals. Do not be discouraged by the numbers. Often, what you need is getting a different marketing strategy and adding something other businesses do not cater for.

Details you have to research about other competitors are:

1. How much do their T-shirts cost?

2. Why and how do they get customers?

3. What is their selling point?

4. Have they been selling well? (So, you'd know what's wrong and what to fix.)

5. What's the quality of their T-shirts?

6. What's their order process?

Stephanie Stephens

After getting everything researched, it's the perfect time for you to map out your plans.

Chapter 4
MAP OUT PLANS

Stephanie Stephens

Draw a business plan, no matter how little you intend to start. According to the article "Five Steps to Getting Your Business Off the Ground" on the Entrepreneur.com website, writing a business plan makes you about twice as likely to actually launch the business. By planning here, what is simply meant is that after you've carried out your research based on the market, the finances, and the competitors, you now have to sort out the best ways and productive steps to penetrate the T-shirt business. How do you intend to get the market rolling? Do you feel you will need a physical

Stephanie Stephens

store? Do you feel doing it completely online is best? Do you want to consider giving coupons? Are you interested in starting an online contest to create a buzz? All these are supposed to be considered in the planning.

Also, you should figure out if you're putting up your T-shirts to other retailers if you'll rather pre-sell if you'll offer shipping and fulfillment of individual T-shirts and other things related to selling your T-shirts.

The best thing here is working on the results of the well carried out research to figure out what will be best for you.

Stephanie Stephens

This also is the point where you're going to decide how well you will spend the capital needed to get the gains needed.

Stephanie Stephens

Chapter 5

SET YOUR GOALS AND OBJECTIVE

Stephanie Stephens

After you've enlightened yourself on how best to start a T-shirt business, it is time to create the finishing line you are running towards. You must set some real goals. You have to consider how many T-shirts you are willing to sell in a year, how many you will love to sell in a particular month, how many you're also willing to sell in a particular week. With the increased level of productivity of the business over time, the goals can be expanded, therefore, it is not a crime to start a little by setting not too difficult goals.

Many people who are new to the business do not understand how important this step is, or, they just don't bother about it. Then, some people will never set goals, not because they don't know they have to but because they are too scared set them because of fear that they may not be able to achieve them.

For a business to be successful, and for it to have a clear picture of what it is working towards, goals must be set. You must set goals and simply believe in your ability to achieve them. This will make you work tirelessly towards achieving them. Just as the law of attraction goes: if you know you're going to reach it, you're going to reach it. Practically put, if you decide now that you want to sell twelve T-shirts every week, if you strongly believe in yourself to achieve it, you will just find yourself doing all it takes to get it achieved, thereby getting your T-shirts moving. If you don't set goals, you may end up having too many lying T-shirts that you were scared to sell.

You can keep track of your goals through Google Drive.

Chapter 6

DETERMINE YOUR BUDGET

Stephanie Stephens

Before deciding to go too deep into this T-shirt business, you must establish a budget. It is true that almost everyone has huge plans but it all comes down to what your budget is. The major thing here is making sure you have enough resources to fulfill your expectations, else, bring down the expectations a bit to what the resources can fulfill. For example, when the budget is so low, the best graphics option for your business may be the cheapest possibility of purchasing royalty-free vectors and creating your own design. The disadvantage that can never be overstated here, however, is that the designs may not be unique, but you have to admit here that they would be a lot cheaper.

Your budget should include some things

- T-shirts samples: You have to budget for this as they will be very much useful to know people's opinions about your T-shirts.

- Purchase of T-shirts: You need to have a budget on how much you will use to purchase the T-shirts. Even if you'll make them yourself, you still have to budget for the materials.

- Printing: If you're going to print your T-shirts yourself, having researched on all it would cost, you must create a budget also for it, and if you'll be contacting a graphics designer to make you a good logo, that should also find its way into your budget.

The totality of budgeting is knowing what you plan on doing, then, getting to know how much everything costs, then, considering how much is available so that adjustments can be made. It should be noted that every other thing can be sacrificed, including quantity, but definitely not quality.

Chapter 7
BRANDING

Stephanie Stephens

What you must come to believe here is that in order for you to mold everything together from the actual T-shirt design to their marketing strategy, you must define your brand. Do not be too confused by the word brand. By brand here, what is meant is your company's personality. By now, you must have figured out how you can stand out, be unique and special based on your niche. Is your company a laid back and happy one to work with or you more formal and reliable? If you plan to have physical stores, what is the experience supposed to be when people get inside it? What are the emotions you want to be felt when people see your T-shirts? Sorting out your brand is sorting out the type of image and emotions you want people to associate with your business. This goes beyond the actual T-shirts people buy from you. It goes as far as how to handle, treat and comment on people's inquiries on Facebook and other social media platforms. For you to get it straight, try striking the assumption that your T-shirts business is a person, what are the characteristics you want to be identified with this person? Define them and show these characteristics to every single marketing platform you may want to have like a website, Facebook page, logo, store, newsletters, e-mails, phone calls, chats etc., everything!

When considering perfect branding, some of its aspects that must come to mind are graphics and web designing, packaging and printing, business name, setting business structure, and employment.

- **GRAPHICS AND WEB DESIGNING.**

Just as you need the perfect logo for your brand and great graphics printing for your shirts, a modern-day seller needs to have a website.

If you are one of the people who are good graphics designer already before having interest in this T-shirt business, you may go ahead to make your own design. However, if you are not a graphics artist, there is need to contact one. Apart from locating them in your locality, there are other platforms on which you can meet them. You can get experts that design logos on **FIVERR** for as low as five dollars. Make sure the person has a good rating and has no pending work because you don't want to wait for weeks before getting your logo. Also, you can get some on other freelance sites like www.guru.com, www.elance.com, www.odesk.com or on T-shirt competition sites like **DesignByHumans**, **Teutonic** or **TeeFury**. The goal is simple, make sure it is the perfect design that you've drawn as a result of your researches and findings that is produced by the graphics designer. Do not settle for anything less. Note that the graphics and slogans used on your T-shirts do not necessarily have to be complex, just make them entirely original and catchy that they can stand undefeatable in a flooded market. You can find great designers also in online design communities like **DRIBBBLE** and **BEHANCE.** What you must not forget is that you must do some research on the Internet to see the latest apparel trends, what the t-shirt community asks for before you make the graphics

Now, the other vital part is the website designing. If you intend to sell directly to consumers, it is a very good idea to have a website. This will tell more about you, give them more access to your business, it can also be an ordering platform, a platform where your T-shirts are displayed. For a good website, ensure you get a great web designer probably on a recommendation. The website should have your logo and represent your brand accurately.

Finally, on design, you must protect it. Just as you are not planning to infringe on another company's copyright or trademark, you must ensure no one takes advantage of yours. Consider protecting your design, logo and/or slogan through copyright or trademark. Uspto.gov

- **PACKAGING AND PRINTING.**

A good number of people come into the T-shirts business because they love screen-printing, are good at it, and have all the necessary equipment. If your situation is other than this, you may decide to search the internet screen printers in your locality and meet with them to discuss your needs. Try as much to interview many of them and work with the best.

Get blank T-shirts for printing from the company you find most appropriate after considering quality and price. If you can make the T-shirts yourself, it is not a bad idea. The printing must be well done because it is on your physical product of which your choice will definitely tell on people's

Stephanie Stephens

perception of your brand. There are some websites that accept t-shirt designs, and they will print these for you on demand. www.Jakprint.com and www.storenvy.com are two great printing companies.

There are numerous types of T-shirts printing, but your decision has to be based on your designs and target market. For example, you can choose from Tultex, American Apparel, Anvil, Next Level, Alstyle, Bella, Bay Island and many others. Also, the thickness of the T-shirts is important when choosing your blank T-shirts. It ranges from 120gr to 200gr, and the ideal is 180gr.

Also, asides the printing, the T-shirt must be well packaged to make it admirable to buyers. No matter how great the printing looks, if the packaging is not complementing it, there would be an adverse result.

- **BUSINESS NAME**

Many people make the mistake of picking a business name without the right steps. It tells on their businesses. For a T-shirt business, your name should reflect your T-shirt, but not limit your ability to expand your T-shirt line. It must be a name that will attract your target market. Also, it must be available, as well as its domain. It looks a bit tiring but it will be summed up for you in three steps.

1. Gather ideas: First, you want to get inspired by how some of your favorite T-shirts brands went about getting their business names. Also, there are great websites that will generate word lists for you, such as www.listofrandomwords.com It is advisable you come up with many

possible options just in case some have been picked.

2. Research on them: This is the point you find out intensively everything about the potential names you have come up with. You have to be interested in what sites and information pop up when you enter your potential names into the search engines. Also, it is important for you to ensure the availability of the domain name so that you will be able to create a website using your brand name. A website that can be helpful with this is www.leandomainsearch.com a website that can predict and score

how effective the name will be is www.networksolutions.com Then, you may need www.wordoid.com to help generate creative words that have available domains. When all attempts fail, get your hands on the Dictionary and Thesaurus to help you coin a name that will have an available domain.

 3. Test your name: It is the final stage of getting the business name. You will have to put the name to a test. You will need some friends and family members to say what they feel about the name. First, you have to make sure the name is not too long or complicated as that will make it hard

to remember. Next, you must ensure the name is readable so that people find it easy to pronounce.

It is important to take all steps to get the best name for your brand. After doing all, bear it in mind that your potential name should be nothing but a strong representation of your T-shirts brand, easy to remember, and available for use. This is highly important because names stick to your business for life. It is not good for business to change names or websites after you are already in business. Great research will help ensure there are no word interpretations or associations

Stephanie Stephens

with your name. It will make people feel good and make them want to buy your T-shirts.

After all, try to trademark your T-shirt brand name as well. This should be done in order to protect it.

- **SETTING BUSINESS STRUCTURE.**

Alongside your business name, what you haven't determined also is your business structure (i.e. sole proprietor or LLC.) In most cases, T-shirts entrepreneurs starting a T-shirt business start as a sole proprietor but with the continuous growth of their company and sales, they change their company's structure to an LLC, LLP or corporation. Think on the big picture of how you want your business to be. How big? How known? Then, you should consult a business or legal professional to help you in sorting out what will be the best and ideal business structure for you.

You also will have to focus on what type of sales you want to be a specialist in. Do you want your business to sell directly to consumers? (Retail) Do you want to sell to other sellers? (Wholesale). Do you want it to be both? This would also go a long way in helping you decide what business structure will be best for you. Check legal zoom, irs.gov

- **EMPLOYMENT**

Also, you have to consider employment. This may not be too difficult if you're planning to run an online store, but then, with an increase in order, you may have to get people for delivery. However, if you're interested in having a physical store, you may need someone to help you with one or two things.

There is no certain number of people you must employ. It depends on you and how you want the business to go.

Even if you want to sell online, if you're the one making the materials, designing the graphics, designing the website, printing the T-shirts, doing the delivery, there is all certainty that your productivity will be low and your services will be delayed. But if you're having a physical store, you have where you but the materials from, you have a graphics designer and a printer, you may decide to start alone since all that is left is selling. Again, it depends on you, how the business is run, and how big you want it to be. Consider hiring interns as an alternative.

Stephanie Stephens

Chapter 8

DROP SHIPPING

Stephanie Stephens

A lot of people starting their T-shirts business start doing so by storing their T-shirts up in their house, in bins, on shelves, in their garage, basement or home office. It depends on what you feel is best for you and what you enjoy doing. Do you feel packing and shipping are not any difficult for you? Do you enjoy it? Is the post office nearby? If all answers are yes, then, storing the T-shirts around yourself is not a bad option. But, if you are not so interested in visiting the post office every day, shipping T-shirts down to people, if you don't have the time or will, or you don't have enough space to store them in your house, then, you can consider hiring a fulfillment house that will take up all the task of storing, packaging and shipping for you for a fee.

Printing T-Shirts at Home
1. Computer
2. Printer
3. Graphic System (Adobe Illustrator)
4. Transfer Paper
5. Heat Press or Screen Printing
6. T-shirts
7. Cutter
8. Storage Space
9. Shipping Equipment (Mailers, Postal Scale, Labels)
10. Time & Money

Chapter 9

ADVERTISING AND MARKETING

Stephanie Stephens

Advertising has over time been known as the soul of business. Even if you have a good design, perfect plan, but lack the right marketing strategy, your target market may be unaware of your T-shirts, and that will send you running at a loss. You must sort a means to spread the word in such a way that those who hear you will go on to spread it too. While may starters rely heavily only on free advertisements for their products, it will not do you good. You must have planned money for advertisement in your budget. You will have to pay for online advertisements and may even have to sponsor some events. Find a perfect way to balance both free and paid promotions. You can choose to advertise your services in a local newspaper and other publications. The advertisement can come both in print and online. You have to bring your target market back to mind here. Place your advertisement on the publications your market target is likely to read. In your advertisement endeavor to mention all the services you render and add an expression that implies to your audience to anticipate more. Create fan pages for your business on social networking sites and include a link to your website. You also can make a trip down to independent clothing stores and department stores to persuade them to sell your design for an agreed profit.

If you are deciding to run the T-shirts business completely online, that you have a website does not automatically means everybody will know about it or find it. It is, therefore, best to work with your web designer to make your website search engine friendly so people can find you easily. Try as much to exchange links with other businesses. Post comments on people's blogs with a link back to your site.

You can create online contests on Instagram and other social media platforms. This will at least cause an interesting mini rush for your T-shirt.

One final advertising technique that also works is wearing your T-shirts as often as you can. This is one of the best means to get your T-shirts seen.

Stephanie Stephens

Chapter 10

PRICING

Stephanie Stephens

This is the point you must be very careful. You can't fix a price that will scare people away because of the added gains you want, yet, you can't fix a price that will not cover your expenses because you want people to rush them. Pricing comes up after you must have reviewed different t-shirt creation options (i.e. online resources and local t-shirt printers) to find out the option better and affordable for you. Everything should be put into consideration here. Starting from the number of color on your design, to the type of printing chosen, to the quality of T-shirt selected. You also must cover other costs like marketing and advertisement. You also must consider who you're selling to. If you're not selling to other stores or on wholesale, you're cutting the middleman, so, that can have an effect on your pricing. The totality of pricing is calculating every dime spent and adding a reasonably expected gain. Then, trying to divide it on the number of products.

Stephanie Stephens

Chapter 11

MAKE SALES

Stephanie Stephens

There are numerous ways to market your new T-shirt, but, they all ball down to remembering your target market and where you can find them. You must understand the best buyer for your T-shirt in terms of gender, age, etc., you must know where you can find them, and you must put your T-shirts in front of them. For example, if your target market is football loving high school students, endeavor to find out where football loving high school students hang out both online and offline.

If you're willing to sell directly to consumers, it is very advisable to have your own website and make provisions for postcards so you can promote your T-shirts business. Afford people the convenience of purchasing the T-shirts directly online. There must be good photography in place to reflect the exact quality of your T-shirts. You also may want to sell your shirts at local events such as flea markets or street fairs or fundraising events.

You can choose to sell to other stores that target your niche market. Stores like these include local boutiques, gift stores, T-shirt shops and even larger retail chain stores. The discovered truth is that many stores prefer supporting businesses in their locality, so it's best to start out with stores in your town or city first.

Stephanie Stephens

CONCLUSION

Starting up a T-shirt business is something that calls for interest, readiness, and focus. If you can give it all it takes, it will offer you all it can. Follow the above steps correctly and I won't be surprised to find myself buying your T-shirts. Let's discussed what you have learned. Let's start with gathering ideas to start the process of starting your own t-shirt business. This is key! Take some time to figure out who you are going to sell your t-shirts to, whether you are printing your shirts at home or will you be using a fulfillment company. Are you using your Hustle Up Journal to keep track of your ideas? Create a plan, come up with a name for your t-shirt brand. Make sure you your name matches your niche and target audience. Now things should be coming together. You have your name let's get it branded with a logo, be sure to hire a professional graphic designer. Now you should be mapping out your plans, setting weekly goals, come up with a budget. Now let's introduce your brand to the world. Create social media pages, choose a drop shipper if you choose this option. Advertise on your social media pages. Now let's start making money.

ABOUT THE BOOK

Have you got an idea or always wanted to start your own T-Shirt business? I have created the perfect guide for you to Hustle Up And Start Your T-Shirt Business. You can learn where to get t-shirt samples to different methods of printing your shirts. Hustle Up and Start your T-Shirt business includes all the guidance you will need to get you started. This book features resources to skyrocket your T shirt business.

Stephanie Stephens

I have taken all my experiences and knowledge to help others start their own T-Shirt business. This book will give you the tools step by step to become the next big thing. The best advice I can give is to just start, stay focus, set goals. In no time you will have your own T-Shirt business.

Stephanie Stephens

Frequently Asked Questions

1. Where do I buy sample shirts?

You can buy sample shirts from

- Customink,
- Printful,
- Zazzle
- Vistaprint

2. How do I set up a business plan? Are there templates?

- Go to sba.gov they will guide you step by step to create the

foundation of your t-shirt business.
3. Where do I buy blank shirts?

- You can buy blank shirts from jiffy shirt.com
- Customink
- Walmart,
- Michaels
- local printer.

4. Where do I find graphic designers?

- Fiver
- Design Crowd
- Freelancer
- Google graphic designers in your area. Consider hiring an intern. Make sure you check reviews,

ratings, and portfolio. Ask for reference if necessary.

5. How do I come up with a Business Name?

- Think Carefully and Research before selecting a name. This will be your brand name that will follow you forever. Your niche should help you come up with a name. Once you have a name conduct a search for name availability in your state to be sure the name hasn't been taken and registered.

6. What is drop shipping?

- Drop Shipping is the easiest way to open an online product store without having any inventory. This means your t shirts will be printed and delivered to your customers with you lifting a finger. Once your customer places an order on your online store the drop shipper will print and ship your order to your customers. This is ideal for beginners. Printful, Teespring are the most popular ones.

7. What sites allow you to create a free website?

- They are hundreds of sites that allow you to create a free website. Some come with different functionalities. I prefer

Shopify. They allow you to try it for 7 days free. There is a monthly fee after the 7 days. There are some really good free sites. I have listed the top sites.

- Wix
- Cafe Press
- GoDaddy
- SquareSpace
- WordPress
- BigCommerce
- BigCartel

8. How do I set up my Business Structure?

- Small Business Administration(SBA)
- Irs.gov

- Legal zoom
- Contact a business attorney

9. How do I get someone to design my website and logo?

There are several affordable web site developers and graphic designers. For Beginners

- Fiverr
- Freelancer
- Shopify
- Big Commerce
- Wix

10. How do I create customizing packaging? Such as T shirt boxes, bags, stickers

- Packlane
- Uline
- The custom box
- Customink
- 4imprints

11. How do I market my t-shirts online?

- Create Contests online via social media
- Sponsor an event within your target audience
- Giveaways
- Reach out to Social Media Influencers & Celebrities
- Wear your own shirts
- Promote your brand on your personal social media pages

- Place Ad in newspaper or magazine

12. How do I trademark my logo and designs?

    - Legal zoom
    - USPTO.gov

13. How do I get my T-shirts printed?

    - You can print them with a local printer in your area or
    - You can choose a fulfillment company that will print and ship your shirts.

14. What do I need to start my t-shirt business from home?

    - Computer
    - Printer

- Graphic Software (Adobe Illustrator)
- Transfer Paper
- Ink
- Heat Press or Screen Printer
- Cutter
- T-shirts.

15. How do I get Started?

    - Just Start! Research

Thank You For Your Purchase!!!!

Thank you for purchasing this book. I hope you were able to gain some knowledge and tools to start your own t-shirt business. Please feel free to leave us a review for this book on Amazon. I would be greatly appreciated. Make sure you check out our T-Shirts email us let us know what you think.

bleszingclothing@gmail.com

Websites:
www.bleszingclothing.com
Facebook:
https://www.facebook.com/bleszingclothing
Instagram:
https://www.instagram.com/bleszing_clothing
Twitter:
https://www.twitter.com/bleszingcloth21

Stephanie Stephens

Thank you & Good Luck

Stephanie Stephens

Stephanie Stephens

Made in United States
North Haven, CT
08 March 2022